The Essential Air Fryer Cookbook

Easy, Mouthwatering and Low-Fat Recipes to Master the Full Potential of Your Air Fryer

Linda Wang

TABLE OF CONTENTS

INTRODUCTION

An Air Fryer is a magic revolutionized kitchen appliance that helps you fry with less or even no oil at all. This kind of product applies Rapid Air technology, which offers a new way to fry with less oil. This new invention cooks food through the circulation of superheated air and generates 80% low-fat food. Although the food is fried with less oil, you don't need to worry as the food processed by the Air Fryer still has the same taste like the food fried using the deep-frying method.

This technology uses a superheated element, which radiates heat close to the food and an exhaust fan in its lid to circulate airflow. An Air Fryer ensures that the food processed is cooked completely. The exhaust fan located at the top of the cooking chamber helps the food get the same heating temperature in every part quickly, resulting in a cooked food of better and healthier quality. Besides, cooking with an Air Fryer is also suitable for those individuals which are too busy or do not have enough time. For example, an Air Fryer only needs half a spoonful of oil and takes 10 minutes to serve a medium bowl of crispy French fries.

In addition to serving healthier food, an Air Fryer also provides some other benefits to you. Since an Air Fryer helps you fry using less oil or without oil for some kind of food, it automatically reduces the fat and cholesterol content in food. Indeed, no one will refuse to enjoy fried food without worrying about the greasy and fat content. Having fried food with no guilt is one of the pleasures of life. Besides having low fat and cholesterol, you save some amount of money by consuming oil sparingly, which can be used for other needs. An Air Fryer also can reheat your food. Sometimes, when you have fried leftover and you reheat it, it will usually serve reheated greasy food with some addition of unhealthy reuse oil. Undoubtedly, the saturated fat in the fried food gets worse because of this process. An Air Fryer helps you reheat your food without being afraid of extra oils that the food may absorb. Fried bananas, fish and chips, nuggets, or even fried chicken can be reheated to become as warm and crispy as they were before by using an Air Fryer.

Some people may think that spending some amount of money to buy a fryer is wasteful. I dare to say that they are wrong because an Air Fryer is not only used to fry. It is a sophisticated multi-function appliance since it also helps you to roast chicken, make steak, grill fish, and even bake a cake. With a built-in air filter, an Air Fryer filters the air and saves your kitchen from smoke and grease.

An air Fryer is really a new innovative method of cooking. Grab it fast and welcome to a clean and healthy kitchen.

also helps you to roast chicken, make steak, grill fish, and even bake a cake. With a built-in air filter, an Air Fryer filters the air and saves your kitchen from smoke and grease.

An air Fryer is really a new innovative method of cooking. Grab it fast and welcome to a clean and healthy kitchen

Parmesan Breakfast Casserole

Preparation Time: 10 minutes

Cooking Time: 20 minutes

Serve: 3

Ingredients:

- 5 eggs
- 2 tbsp heavy cream

- 2 tbsp parmesan cheese, grated
- 3 tbsp chunky tomato sauce

Directions:

1. Preheat the air fryer to 325 ^{0}F.
2. In mixing bowl, combine together cream and eggs.
3. Add cheese and tomato sauce and mix well.
4. Spray air fryer baking dish with cooking spray.
5. Pour mixture into baking dish and place in the air fryer basket.
6. Cook for 20 minutes.
7. Serve and enjoy.

Nutrition:

Calories 185, Fat 14 g, Carbohydrates 2 g, Sugar 1.2 g, Protein 13.6 g,Cholesterol 290 mg

Mushrooms and Cheese Spread

Preparation Time: 25 minutes

Servings: 4

Ingredients:

- ¼ cup mozzarella; shredded
- 1 cup white mushrooms
- ½ cup coconut cream
- A pinch of salt and black pepper

- Cooking spray

Directions:

1. Put the mushrooms in your air fryer's basket, grease with cooking spray and cook at 370 °F for 20 minutes.
2. Transfer to a blender, add the remaining ingredients, pulse well, divide into bowls and serve as a spread

Nutrition:

Calories: 202; Fat: 12g; Fiber: 2g; Carbs: 5g; Protein: 7g

Indian Cauliflower

Preparation Time: 10 minutes

Cooking Time: 20 minutes

Serve: 2

Ingredients:

- 3 cups cauliflower florets
- 2 tsp fresh lemon juice
- ½ tbsp ginger paste
- 2 tbsp water
- 1 tsp chili powder
- ¼ tsp turmeric
- ½ cup vegetable stock
- Salt
- Pepper

Directions:

1. Add all ingredients into the air fryer baking dish and mix well.

2. Place dish in the air fryer and cook at 400 ^{0}F for 10 minutes.
3. Stir well and cook at 360 ^{0}F for 10 minutes more.
4. Stir well and serve.

Nutrition:

Calories 49, Fat 0.5 g, Carbohydrates 9 g, Sugar 3 g, Protein 3 g, Cholesterol 0 mg

Sweet Potato Hash

Preparation Time: 10 minutes

Cooking Time: 15 minutes

Servings: 6

Ingredients:

- 2 large sweet potato, cut into small cubes
- 2 slices bacon, cut into small pieces
- 1 tablespoon smoked paprika
- 2 tablespoons olive oil
- 1 teaspoon sea salt
- 1 teaspoon ground black pepper
- 1 teaspoon dried dill weed

Directions:

1. Preheat the Air Fryer to 400 degree F and grease an Air fryer pan.
2. Mix together sweet potato, bacon, olive oil, paprika, salt, black pepper and dill in a large bowl.

3. Transfer the mixture into the preheated air fryer pan and cook for about 15 minutes, stirring in between.
4. Dish out and serve warm.

Nutrition:

Calories: 191, Fat: 6g, Carbohydrates: 31.4g, Sugar: 6g, Protein: 3.7g, Sodium: 447mg

Artichoke Omelet

Preparation Time: 20 minutes

Servings: 2

Ingredients:

- 6 eggs; whisked
- 3 artichoke hearts; canned, drained and chopped.
- 2 tbsp. avocado oil

- 1/2 tsp. oregano; dried
- Salt and black pepper to taste

Directions:

1. In a bowl, mix all ingredients except the oil; stir well. Add the oil to your air fryer's pan and heat it up at 320 °F.
2. Add the egg mixture, cook for 15 minutes, divide between plates and serve

Potato Frittata

Preparation Time: 25 minutes

Servings: 6

Ingredients:

- 1 lb. small potatoes; chopped.
- 2 red onions; chopped.
- 1 oz. parmesan cheese; grated
- 1/2 cup heavy cream

- 8 eggs; whisked
- 1 tbsp. olive oil
- Salt and black pepper to taste

Directions:

1. In a bowl, mix all ingredients except the potatoes and oil; stir well.
2. Heat up your air fryer's pan with the oil at 320 °F. Add the potatoes, stir and cook for 5 minutes
3. Add the egg mixture, spread and cook for 15 minutes more. Divide the frittata between plates and serve

Paprika Cod

Preparation Time: 17 minutes

Servings: 4

Ingredients:

- 1 lb. cod fillets, boneless, skinless and cubed
- 2 cups baby arugula

- 1 spring onion; chopped.
- 2 tbsp. fresh cilantro; minced
- ½ tsp. oregano, ground
- ½ tsp. sweet paprika
- A drizzle of olive oil
- Salt and black pepper to taste.

Directions:

1. Take a bowl and mix the cod with salt, pepper, paprika, oregano and the oil, toss, transfer the cubes to your air fryer's basket and cook at 360°F for 12 minutes
2. In a salad bowl, mix the cod with the remaining ingredients, toss, divide between plates and serve.

Nutrition:

Calories: 240; Fat: 11g; Fiber: 3g; Carbs: 5g; Protein: 8g

Awesome Tartar Sauce Chips

Preparation Time: 55 minutes

Servings: 2

Ingredients:

- 2 potatoes [large]
- 2 cloves garlic [crushed]
- 1 teaspoon rosemary
- 1 tablespoon oil [olive]

Sauce:

- 1 shallot [chopped]
- 3 tablespoon capers [drained; chopped]
- 2 tablespoon jalapenos [drained; chopped]
- 1 squeeze lemon juice
- 3 tablespoon parsley [fresh; chopped]
- 1 cup mayonnaise
- salt and pepper to taste

Directions:

1. Cut potatoes into wedges and soak in salted water for about 20 minutes.
2. Preheat Air Fryer to 350 - degrees Fahrenheit.
3. Mix all the ingredients and coat it over the potatoes. Cook the coated potatoes for about 25 minutes.
4. Make a sauce and serve with it. Enjoy the delicious taste.

Nutritious Salmon

Preparation Time: 10 minutes

Cooking Time: 10 minutes

Serve: 2

Ingredients:

- 2 salmon fillets
- 1/4 tsp ground cardamom
- 1 tbsp olive oil
- 1/2 tsp paprika
- Salt

Directions:

1. Preheat the air fryer to 350 ^{0}F.
2. Coat the salmon fillets with olive oil and season with paprika, cardamom and salt and place into the air fryer basket.
3. Cook salmon for 10-12 minutes. Turn halfway through.
4. Serve and enjoy.

Nutrition:

Calories 160, Fat 1 g, Carbohydrates 1 g, Sugar 0.5 g, Protein 22 g, Cholesterol 60 mg

Coconut Crusted Shrimp

Preparation Time: 15 minutes

Cooking Time: 40 minutes

Servings: 3

Ingredients:

- 8 ounces coconut milk
- ½ cup panko breadcrumbs
- ½ cup sweetened coconut, shredded
- 1 pound large shrimp, peeled and deveined
- Salt and black pepper, to taste

Directions:

1. Preheat the Air fryer to 350 degrees F and grease an Air fryer basket.
2. Place the coconut milk in a shallow bowl.
3. Mix coconut, breadcrumbs, salt and black pepper in another bowl.
4. Dip each shrimp into coconut milk and finally, dredge in the coconut mixture.

5. Arrange half of the shrimps into the Air fryer basket and cook for about 20 minutes.
6. Dish out the shrimps onto serving plates and repeat with the remaining mixture to serve.

Nutrition:

Calories: 408, Fats: 23.7g, Carbohydrates: 11.7g, Sugar: 3.4g, Proteins: 31g, Sodium: 253mg

Lemony and Spicy Coconut Crusted Salmon

Preparation Time: 10 minutes

Cooking Time: 6 minutes

Servings: 4

Ingredients:

- 2 egg whites
- 1 pound salmon
- ½ cup flour
- ½ cup breadcrumbs
- ¼ teaspoon lemon zest
- ½ cup unsweetened coconut, shredded
- Salt and freshly ground black pepper, to taste
- ¼ teaspoon cayenne pepper
- ¼ teaspoon red pepper flakes, crushed
- Vegetable oil, as required

Directions:

1. Preheat the Air fryer to 400 degrees F and grease an Air fryer basket.
2. Mix the flour, salt and black pepper in a shallow dish.
3. Whisk the egg whites in a second shallow dish.
4. Mix the breadcrumbs, coconut, lime zest, salt and cayenne pepper in a third shallow dish.
5. Coat salmon in the flour, then dip in the egg whites and then into the breadcrumb mixture evenly.
6. Place the salmon in the Air fryer basket and drizzle with vegetable oil.
7. Cook for about 6 minutes and dish out to serve warm.

Nutrition:

Calories: 558, Fat: 22.2g, Carbohydrates: 18.6g, Sugar: 8.7g, Protein: 43g, Sodium: 3456mg

Fish and Salsa

Preparation Time: 20 minutes

Servings: 4

Ingredients:

- 4 sea bass fillets; boneless
- 3 tomatoes; roughly chopped.
- 3 garlic cloves; minced

- 2 spring onions; chopped.
- 1 tbsp. balsamic vinegar
- ¼ cup chicken stock
- 1 tbsp. olive oil
- A pinch of salt and black pepper

Directions:

1. In a blender, combine all the ingredients except the fish and pulse well.
2. Put the mix in a pan that fits the air fryer, add the fish, toss gently, introduce the pan in the fryer and cook at 380 °F for 15 minutes. Divide between plates and serve.

Nutrition:

Calories: 261; Fat: 11g; Fiber: 4g; Carbs: 7g; Protein: 11g

Black Sea Bass with Rosemary Vinaigrette

Preparation Time: 17 minutes

Servings: 4

Ingredients:

- 4 black sea bass fillets; boneless and skin scored
- 3 garlic cloves; minced
- 1 tbsp. rosemary; chopped.
- 2 tbsp. olive oil
- 3 tbsp. black olives, pitted and chopped.
- A pinch of salt and black pepper
- Juice of 1 lime

Directions:

1. Take a bowl and mix the oil with the olives and the rest of the ingredients except the fish and whisk well.

2. Place the fish in a pan that fits the air fryer, spread the rosemary vinaigrette all over.
3. Put the pan in the machine and cook at 380 °F for 12 minutes, flipping the fish halfway. Divide between plates and serve

Nutrition:

Calories: 220; Fat: 12g; Fiber: 4g; Carbs: 6g; Protein: 10g

Tuna Zoodle Casserole

Preparation Time: 30 minutes

Servings: 4

Ingredients:

- 1 oz. pork rinds, finely ground
- 2 medium zucchini, spiralized
- ¼ cup diced white onion
- 2: 5-oz.cans albacore tuna
- ¼ cup chopped white mushrooms
- 2 stalks celery, finely chopped
- ½ cup heavy cream
- 2 tbsp. salted butter
- ½ cup vegetable broth
- 2 tbsp. full-fat mayonnaise
- ½ tsp. red pepper flakes
- ¼ tsp. xanthan gum

Directions:

1. In a large saucepan over medium heat, melt butter. Add onion, mushrooms and celery and sauté until fragrant, about 3–5 minutes.
2. Pour in heavy cream, vegetable broth, mayonnaise and xanthan gum. Reduce heat and continue cooking an additional 3 minutes, until the mixture begins to thicken
3. Add red pepper flakes, zucchini and tuna. Turn off heat and stir until zucchini noodles are coated
4. Pour into 4-cup round baking dish. Top with ground pork rinds and cover the top of the dish with foil. Place into the air fryer basket. Adjust the temperature to 370 Degrees F and set the timer for 15 minutes.
5. When 3 minutes remain, remove the foil to brown the top of the casserole. Serve warm.

Nutrition:

Calories: 339; Protein: 19.7g; Fiber: 1.8g; Fat: 25.1g; Carbs: 6.1g

Grilled Shrimp

Preparation time: 15 minutes

Servings: 4

Ingredients:

- Medium shrimp/prawns: 8
- Melted butter: 1 tbsp.
- Pepper and salt: as desired
- Rosemary: 1 sprig
- Minced garlic cloves: 3

Directions:

1. Combine all of the fixings in a mixing bowl. Toss well and arrange in the fryer basket.
2. Set the timer for 7 minutes: 356º Fahrenheit and serve.

Halibut and Sun Dried Tomatoes

Preparation Time: 20 Minutes

Servings: 2

Ingredients:

- 2 medium halibut fillets
- 9 black olives; pitted and sliced
- 2 garlic cloves; minced
- 6 sun dried tomatoes; chopped

- 2 small red onions; sliced
- 4 rosemary springs; chopped
- 1 fennel bulb; sliced
- 1/2 tsp. red pepper flakes; crushed
- 2 tsp. olive oil
- Salt and black pepper to the taste

Directions:

1. Season fish with salt, pepper, rub with garlic and oil and put in a heat proof dish that fits your air fryer.
2. Add onion slices, sun dried tomatoes, fennel, olives, rosemary and sprinkle pepper flakes, transfer to your air fryer and cook at 380°F, for 10 minutes. Divide fish and veggies on plates and serve

Sweet Chicken Kabobs

Preparation Time: 20 minutes

Cooking Time: 14 minutes

Servings: 3

Ingredients:

- 4 scallions, chopped
- 2 teaspoons sesame seeds, toasted
- 1 pound chicken tenders
- 1 tablespoon fresh ginger, finely grated
- Wooden skewers, pres oaked
- 4 garlic cloves, minced
- ½ cup soy sauce
- ½ cup pineapple juice
- ¼ cup sesame oil
- A pinch of black pepper

Directions:

1. Preheat the Air fryer to 390 degrees F and grease an Air fryer pan.

2. Mix scallion, ginger, garlic, pineapple juice, soy sauce, oil, sesame seeds, and black pepper in a large baking dish.
3. Thread chicken tenders onto pre-soaked wooden skewers.
4. Coat the skewers generously with marinade and refrigerate for about 2 hours.
5. Transfer half of the skewers in the Air fryer pan and cook for about 7 minutes.
6. Repeat with the remaining mixture and dish out to serve warm.

Nutrition:

Calories: 392, Fat: 23g, Carbohydrates: 9.9g, Sugar: 4.1g, Protein: 35.8g, Sodium: 1800mg

Buttered Duck Breasts

Preparation Time: 15 minutes

Cooking Time: 22 minutes

Servings: 4

Ingredients:

- 2: 12-ouncesduck breasts
- 3 tablespoons unsalted butter, melted
- ½ teaspoon dried thyme, crushed
- ¼ teaspoon star anise powder
- Salt and ground black pepper, as required

Directions:

1. Preheat the Air fryer to 390 degrees F and grease an Air fryer basket.
2. Season the duck breasts generously with salt and black pepper.
3. Arrange the duck breasts into the prepared Air fryer basket and cook for about 10 minutes.

4. Dish out the duck breasts and drizzle with melted butter.
5. Season with thyme and star anise powder and place the duck breasts again into the Air fryer basket.
6. Cook for about 12 more minutes and dish out to serve warm.

Nutrition:

Calories: 296, Fat: 15.5g, Carbohydrates: 0.1g, Sugar: 0g, Protein: 37.5g, Sodium: 100mg

Duck Breast and Potatoes

Preparation Time: 40 minutes

Servings: 2

Ingredients:

- 1 duck breast; halved and scored
- 2 tbsp. butter; melted
- 1 oz. red wine
- 2 gold potatoes; cubed

- Salt and black pepper to taste

Directions:

1. Season the duck pieces with salt and pepper, put them in a pan and heat up over medium-high heat.
2. Cook for 4 minutes on each side, transfer to your air fryer's basket and cook at 360 °F for 8 minutes
3. Put the butter in a pan and heat it up over medium heat; then add the potatoes, salt, pepper and the wine and cook for 8 minutes
4. Add the duck pieces, toss and cook everything for 3-4 minutes more. Divide all between plates and serve.

Sage Beef

Preparation time: 10 minutes

Cooking time: 30 minutes

Servings: 4

Ingredients:

- 2pounds beef stew meat, cubed
- 2tablespoons butter, melted
- 1tablespoon sage, chopped

- ½ teaspoon coriander, ground
- ½ tablespoon garlic powder
- 1teaspoon Italian seasoning
- Salt and black pepper to the taste

Directions:

1. In the air fryer's pan, mix the beef with the sage, melted butter and the other ingredients, introduce the pan in the fryer and cook at 360 degrees F for 30 minutes.
2. Divide everything between plates and serve.

Nutrition:

Calories 290, Fat 11, Fiber 6, Carbs 20, Protein 29

Venetian Liver

Preparation time: 10-20;

Cooking time: 15-30;

Serve: 6

Ingredients:

- 500g veal liver
- 2 white onions

- 2 tbsp vinegar
- 100g of water
- Salt and pepper to taste

Directions:

1. Chop the onion and put it inside the pan with the water. Set the air fryer to 180 °C and cook for 20 minutes.
2. Add the liver cut into small pieces and vinegar, close the lid, and cook for an additional 10 minutes.
3. Add salt and pepper.

Nutrition:

Calories 131, Fat 14.19 g, Carbohydrates 16.40 g, Sugars 5.15 g, Protein 25.39 g, Cholesterol 350.41 mg

Creamy Beef

Preparation Time: 55 minutes

Servings: 4

Ingredients:

- 1½ lbs. cubed beef
- 4 oz. brown mushrooms; sliced
- 1 red onion; chopped.
- 2½ tbsp. vegetable oil
- 2 garlic cloves; minced
- 1½ tbsp. white flour
- 1 tbsp. cilantro; chopped.
- 8 oz. sour cream
- Salt and black pepper to taste

Directions:

1. In a bowl, mix the beef with the salt, pepper and flour; toss.
2. Heat up the oil in a pan that fits your air fryer over medium-high heat.

3. Add the beef, onions and garlic; stir and cook for 5 minutes
4. Add the mushrooms and toss
5. Place the pan in the fryer and cook at 380°F for 35 minutes
6. Add the sour cream and cilantro and toss; cook for 5 minutes more. Divide everything between plates and serve.

Pork Tenderloin with Bacon & Veggies

Servings: 3

Preparation Time: 20 minutes

Cooking Time: 28 minutes

Ingredients

- 3 potatoes
- 6 bacon slices
- ¾ pound frozen green beans
- 3: 6-ouncespork tenderloins
- 2 tablespoons olive oil

Directions:

1. Set the temperature of air fryer to 390 degrees F. Grease an air fryer basket.
2. With a fork, pierce the potatoes.
3. Place potatoes into the prepared air fryer basket and air fry for about 15 minutes.
4. Wrap one bacon slice around 4-6 green beans.
5. Coat the pork tenderloins with oil

6. After 15 minutes, add the pork tenderloins into air fryer basket with potatoes and air fry for about 5-6 minutes.
7. Remove the pork tenderloins from the basket.
8. Place bean rolls into the basket and top with the pork tenderloins.
9. Air fry for another 7 minutes.
10. Remove from air fryer and transfer the pork tenderloins onto a platter.
11. Cut each tenderloin into desired size slices.
12. Serve alongside the potatoes and green beans rolls.

Nutrition:

Calories: 918, Carbohydrate: 42.4g, Protein: 77.9g, Fat: 47.7g, Sugar: 4g, Sodium: 1400mg

Herbs Crumbed Rack of Lamb

Servings: 5

Preparation Time: 20 minutes

Cooking Time: 30 minutes

Ingredients

- 1 egg
- 1 tablespoon butter, melted
- ½ cup panko breadcrumbs
- 1 garlic clove, finely chopped
- 1¾ pounds rack of lamb
- Salt and ground black pepper, as required
- 1 tablespoon fresh thyme, minced
- 1 tablespoon fresh rosemary, minced

Directions:

1. In a bowl, mix together the butter, garlic, salt, and black pepper.
2. Coat the rack of lamb evenly with garlic mixture.
3. In a shallow dish, beat the egg.
4. In another dish, mix together the breadcrumbs and herbs.
5. Dip the rack of lamb in beaten egg and then, coat with breadcrumbs mixture.
6. Set the temperature of air fryer to 212 degrees F. Grease an air fryer basket.

7. Place the rack of lamb into the prepared air fryer basket.
8. Air Fry for about 25 minutes and then 5 more minutes at 390 degrees F.
9. Remove from air fryer and place the rack of lamb onto a cutting board for about 5 minutes
10. With a sharp knife, cut the rack of lamb into individual chops and serve.

Nutrition:

Calories: 277, Carbohydrate: 5.9g, Protein: 28.6g, Fat: 14.6g, Sugar: 0.2g, Sodium: 191mg

Sweet and Spicy Cauliflower

Preparation Time: 15 minutes

Cooking Time: 25 minutes

Servings: 4

Ingredients:

- 1 head cauliflower, cut into florets
- 2 scallions, chopped
- ¾ cup onion, thinly sliced
- 5 garlic cloves, finely sliced
- 1 tablespoon hot sauce
- 1 tablespoon rice vinegar
- 1½ tablespoons soy sauce
- 1 teaspoon coconut sugar
- Pinch of red pepper flakes
- Ground black pepper, as required

Directions:

1. Preheat the Air fryer to 350 degrees F and grease an Air fryer basket.

2. Arrange the cauliflower florets into the Air fryer basket and cook for about 10 minutes.
3. Add the onions and garlic and cook for 10 more minutes.
4. Meanwhile, mix soy sauce, hot sauce, vinegar, coconut sugar, red pepper flakes, and black pepper in a bowl.
5. Pour the soy sauce mixture into the cauliflower mixture.
6. Cook for about 5 minutes and dish out onto serving plates.
7. Garnish with scallions and serve warm.

Nutrition:

Calories: 72, Fat: 0.2g, Carbohydrates: 13.8g, Sugar: 3.1g, Protein: 3.6g, Sodium: 1300mg

Tofu with Peanut Butter Sauce

Preparation Time: 20 minutes

Cooking Time: 15 minutes

Servings: 3

Ingredients:

For Tofu

- 1: 14-ounces block tofu, pressed and cut into strips
- 6 bamboo skewers, pre-soaked and halved

For Tofu

- 2 tablespoons soy sauce
- 2 tablespoons fresh lime juice
- 1 tablespoon maple syrup
- 1 teaspoon Sriracha sauce
- 2 teaspoons fresh ginger, peeled
- 2 garlic cloves, peeled

For Sauce

- 2 garlic cloves, peeled
- 1: 2-inches piece fresh ginger, peeled
- ½ cup creamy peanut butter

- 1 tablespoon soy sauce
- 1 tablespoon fresh lime juice
- 1-2 teaspoons Sriracha sauce
- 6 tablespoons of water

Directions:

1. Preheat the Air fryer to 370 degrees F and grease an Air fryer basket.
2. Put all the ingredients except tofu in a food processor and pulse until smooth.
3. Transfer the mixture into a bowl and marinate tofu in it.
4. Thread one tofu strip onto each little bamboo stick and arrange them in the Air fryer basket.
5. Cook for about 15 minutes and dish out onto serving plates.
6. Mix all the ingredients for the sauce in a food processor and pulse until smooth.
7. Drizzle the sauce over tofu and serve warm.

Nutrition:

Calories: 385, Fats: 27.3g, Carbohydrates: 9.3g, Sugar: 9.1g, Proteins: 23g, Sodium: 1141mg

Cheesy Mushroom Pizza

Servings: 2

Preparation Time: 15 minutes

Cooking Time: 6 minutes

Ingredients

- 2 Portobello mushroom caps, stemmed
- 2 tablespoons olive oil
- 1/8 teaspoon dried Italian seasonings
- 2 tablespoons canned tomatoes, chopped
- 2 tablespoons mozzarella cheese, shredded
- 2 Kalamata olives, pitted and sliced
- 2 tablespoons Parmesan cheese, grated freshly
- Salt, to taste
- 1 teaspoon red pepper flakes, crushed

Directions:

1. Set the temperature of air fryer to 320 degrees F. Grease an air fryer basket.
2. With a spoon, scoop out the center of each mushroom cap.

3. Coat each mushroom cap with oil from both sides.
4. Sprinkle the inside of caps with Italian seasoning and salt.
5. Place the canned tomato evenly over both caps, followed by the olives and mozzarella cheese.
6. Arrange mushroom caps into the prepared air fryer basket.
7. Air fry for about 5-6 minutes.
8. Remove from air fryer and immediately sprinkle with the Parmesan cheese and red pepper flakes.
9. Serve.

Nutrition:

Calories: 251, Carbohydrate: 5.7g, Protein: 13.4g, Fat: 21g, Sugar: 0.7g, Sodium: 330mg

Lemony Green Beans

Servings: 3

Preparation Time: 15 minutes

Cooking Time: 12 minutes

Ingredients

- 1 pound green beans, trimmed and halved
- 1 teaspoon butter, melted
- ¼ teaspoon garlic powder
- 1 tablespoon fresh lemon juice
- Salt and ground black pepper, as required

Directions:

1. In a large bowl, add all the ingredients and toss to coat well.
2. Set the temperature of air fryer to 400 degrees F. Grease an air fryer basket.
3. Arrange green beans into the prepared air fryer basket.
4. Air fry for about 10-12 minutes.

5. Remove from air fryer and transfer the green beans onto serving plates.
6. Serve hot.

Nutrition:

Calories: 60, Carbohydrate: 11.1g, Protein: 2.8g, Fat: 1.5g, Sugar: 2.3g, Sodium: 70mg

Rice & Beans Stuffed Bell Peppers

Servings: 5

Preparation Time: 15 minutes

Cooking Time: 15 minutes

Ingredients

- ½ small bell pepper, seeded and chopped
- 1 cup cooked rice
- ½ cup mozzarella cheese, shredded
- 1: 15-ouncescan diced tomatoes with juice
- 1: 15-ouncescan red kidney beans, rinsed and drained
- 1½ teaspoons Italian seasoning
- 5 large bell peppers, tops removed and seeded
- 1 tablespoon Parmesan cheese, grated

Directions:

1. In a bowl, mix well chopped bell pepper, tomatoes with juice, beans, rice, and Italian seasoning.

2. Stuff each bell pepper evenly with the rice mixture.
3. Set the temperature of air fryer to 360 degrees F. Grease an air fryer basket.
4. Arrange bell peppers into the air fryer basket in a single layer.
5. Air fry for about 12 minutes.
6. Meanwhile, in a bowl, mix together the mozzarella and Parmesan cheese.
7. Remove the air fryer basket and top each bell pepper with cheese mixture.
8. Air fry for 3 more minutes.
9. Remove from air fryer and transfer the bell peppers onto a serving platter.
10. Set aside to cool slightly.
11. Serve warm.

Nutrition:

Calories: 288, Carbohydrate: 55g, Protein: 11.3g, Fat: 3.1g, Sugar: 9.7g, Sodium: 286mg

Greek Vegetable Soup

Preparation Time: 15 minutes

Cooking Time: 40 minutes

Servings: 4

Ingredients:

- 3 tablespoons of olive oil
- 1 onion, chopped
- 1 clove garlic, minced
- 2 medium carrots, chopped
- 3 cups of cabbage, shredded
- 2 celery stocks, chopped
- 2 cups of cooked chickpeas
- 4 cups of vegetable broth
- 15-ounce fire-roasted tomatoes, diced
- salt and pepper to taste

Directions:

1. Put the olive oil in the air fryer and set to medium heat saute.

2. Add the onions and cook until soft. Add garlic and cabbage and cook for another 5 minutes. When the cabbage softens, add the carrots, celery, and chickpeas. Stir everything to combine and cook for 5 minutes longer
3. Add the broth and canned tomatoes, then season with salt and pepper.
4. Press cancel to end saute mode and cover the pot with the lid set to sealing mode.
5. Set to soup mode and adjust the time to 10 minutes.
6. After completion, release the pressure manually and serve immediately.
7. You may garnish the soup with parsley, feta, or anything you like on soup

Nutrition:

Calories - 412.9 Protein - 6.3 g. Fat - 26.1 g. Carbs - 43.2 g.

Crushed Lentil Soup

Preparation Time: 10 minutes

Cooking Time: 30 minutes

Servings: 8

Ingredients:

- 2 tablespoons vegetable broth
- 1 onion, finely chopped
- 4 garlic cloves, minced
- 2 cups red split lentils
- 4 cups unsalted vegetable broth
- 2 cups of water
- 1 small pinch saffron
- 1 teaspoon cumin
- 1 teaspoon coriander
- ½ teaspoon freshly ground black pepper
- 1 teaspoon sea salt
- ½ teaspoon of red pepper flakes
- 2 bay leaves
- 2 tablespoons fresh lemon juice

Directions:

1. Put the air fryer to saute, add the vegetable broth, 2 tablespoons. Then put in the garlic and onions and cook until they are soft, about 4-5 minutes.
2. Add remaining ingredients except for bay leaves and lemon juice. Stir and then lock the lid of the air fryer.
3. Press cancel and choose the soup function. Set timer for 30 minutes. After the 30 minutes, let it sit for another 20 minutes to release the pressure.
4. Open the lid and add bay leaves and lemon juice, then stir for 5 minutes.
5. Remove bay leaves and serve.

Nutrition:

Calories – 191 Protein – 11.8 g. Fat – 1.2 g. Carbs – 34.4 g.

Air fryer Minestrone Soup

Preparation Time: 10 minutes

Cooking Time: 35 minutes

Servings: 6

Ingredients:

- 2 tablespoons olive oil
- 3 cloves garlic, minced
- 1 onion, diced
- 2 celery stalks, diced
- 2 carrots, peeled and diced
- 1 ½ teaspoons fresh basil
- 28 ounce can tomatoes, diced
- 1 teaspoon dried oregano
- ½ teaspoon fennel seed
- 6 cups low-sodium chicken broth
- 1 can kidney beans, drained and rinsed
- 1 zucchini, chopped
- 1 Parmesan rind
- 1 bay leaf
- 1 bunch kale, chopped and stems removed

- 2 teaspoons red wine vinegar
- kosher salt and freshly ground black pepper
- ⅓ cup Parmesan, grated
- 2 tablespoons fresh parsley leaves, chopped

Directions:

1. Set air fryer to saute, add olive oil, garlic, onion, carrots, and celery. Cook, occasionally stirring, until tender. Stir in basil, oregano, and fennel seeds, for a minute, until fragrant.
2. Pour in the chicken stock, tomatoes, kidney beans, zucchini, parmesan rind, and bay leaf. Select the manual high pressure setting and set for 5 minutes.
3. When completed, press quick release to remove all pressure.
4. Stir in the kale for about 2 minutes, then stir in red wine vinegar and season with salt and pepper to taste. Ready to serve.

Nutrition:

Calories – 227 Protein – 14 g. Fat – 7 g. Carbs – 26 g.

Sesame Seeds Bok Choy (Vegan)

Preparation Time: 10 minutes

Cooking Time: 6 minutes

Servings: 4

Ingredients:

- 4 bunches baby bok choy, bottoms removed and leaves separated
- 1 teaspoon sesame seeds

- 1 teaspoon garlic powder
- Olive oil cooking spray

Directions:

1. Preheat the Air fryer to 325 ^{0}F and grease an Air fryer basket.
2. Arrange the bok choy leaves into the Air fryer basket and spray with the cooking spray.
3. Sprinkle with garlic powder and cook for about 6 minutes, shaking twice in between.
4. Dish out in the bok choy onto serving plates and serve garnished with sesame seeds.

Nutrition:

Calories: 26, Fat: 0.7g, Carbohydrates: 4g, Sugar: 1.9g, Protein: 2.5g, Sodium: 98mg

Basil Tomatoes (Vegan)

Servings: 2

Preparation Time: 10 minutes

Cooking Time: 10 minutes

Ingredients

- 2 tomatoes, halved
- 1 tablespoon fresh basil, chopped
- Olive oil cooking spray
- Salt and ground black pepper, as required

Directions:

1. Set the temperature of air fryer to 320 degrees F. Grease an air fryer basket.
2. Spray the tomato halves evenly with cooking spray and sprinkle with salt, black pepper and basil.
3. Arrange tomato halves into the prepared air fryer basket, cut sides up.

4. Air fry for about 10 minutes or until desired doneness.
5. Remove from air fryer and transfer the tomatoes onto serving plates.
6. Serve warm.

Nutrition:

Calories: 22, Carbohydrate: 4.8g, Protein: 1.1g, Fat: 4.8g, Sugar: 3.2g, Sodium: 84mg

Grilled Jerk Chicken

Servings: 8

Cooking Time: 60 minutes

Ingredients:

- 4 habanero chilies
- 8 pieces chicken legs
- 5 cloves of garlic, minced
- ¾ malt vinegar

- ¾ soy sauce
- 2 tablespoons rum
- 2tablespoon salt
- 2 ½ teaspoons ground allspice
- 1 ½ teaspoons ground nutmeg
- ¾ ground cloves

Directions

1. Place all ingredients in a Ziploc bag and give a good shake. Allow marinating in the fridge for at least 2 hours.
2. Preheat the air fryer at 375 degrees F.
3. Place the grill pan accessory in the air fryer.
4. Grill the chicken for 60 minutes and flip the chicken every 10 minutes for even grilling.

Nutrition

Calories: 204; Carbs: 1.2g; Protein:28.7 g; Fat: 8.1g

Chili and Yogurt Marinated Chicken

Servings: 3

Cooking Time: 40 minutes

Ingredients:

- 7 dried chilies, seeds removed and broken into pieces
- 4 cloves of garlic, minced
- 1-inch ginger, peeled and chopped
- ½ cup whole milk yogurt
- 3 tablespoons fresh lime juice
- 1 tablespoon smoked paprika
- 2 tablespoons prepared mustard
- 1 tablespoon ground coriander
- 1 ½ teaspoon garam masala
- ½ teaspoon ground cumin
- 1 ½ pounds skinless chicken thighs
- Salt and pepper to taste

Directions

1. Place all ingredients in a Ziploc bag and give a good shake to combine everything.
2. Allow marinating for at least 2 hours in the fridge.
3. Preheat the air fryer at 375 degrees F.
4. Place the grill pan accessory in the air fryer.
5. Grill for at least 40 minutes.
6. Make sure to flip the chicken every 10 minutes.

Nutrition

Calories: 583; Carbs: 25.5g; Protein:54.6 g; Fat: 29.8g

Grilled Chicken with Scallions

Servings: 4

Cooking Time: 1 hour

Ingredients:

- 2 pounds whole chicken
- Salt and pepper to taste
- 2 cloves of garlic, peeled and crushed
- 4 sprigs rosemary
- 2 bunches scallions

Directions

1. Season the whole chicken with salt and pepper.
2. Place inside the chicken cavity the rosemary, garlic, and scallions.
3. Preheat the air fryer at 375 degrees F.
4. Place the grill pan accessory in the air fryer.
5. Grill the chicken for 1 hour.

Nutrition

Calories: 470; Carbs: 46.2g; Protein: 37.2g; Fat: 15.9g

Crab Balls

Preparation Time: 25 minutes

Servings: 8

Ingredients:

- 16 oz. lump crabmeat; chopped.
- 2/3 cup almond meal

- 1 egg; whisked
- ½ cup coconut cream
- 2 tbsp. chives, mined
- 1 tsp. mustard
- 1 tsp. lemon juice
- A pinch of salt and black pepper
- Cooking spray

Directions:

1. Take a bowl and mix all the ingredients except the cooking spray and stir well.
2. Shape medium balls out of this mix, place them in the fryer and cook at 390 °F for 20 minutes

Nutrition:

Calories: 141; Fat: 7g; Fiber: 2g; Carbs: 4g; Protein: 9g

Feta Cheese Dip

Preparation Time: 10 minutes

Servings: 6

Ingredients:

- 2 avocados, peeled, pitted and mashed
- 1 garlic clove; minced
- ¼ cup spring onion; chopped.

- 1 tbsp. jalapeno; minced
- ¼ cup parsley; chopped.
- ½ cup feta cheese, crumbled
- Juice of 1 lime

Directions:

1. In a ramekin, mix all the ingredients and whisk them well.
2. Introduce in the fryer and cook at 380 °F for 5 minutes. Serve as a party dip right away

Nutrition:

Calories: 200; Fat: 12g; Fiber: 2g; Carbs: 4g; Protein: 9g

Cheese Stuffed Tomatoes

Preparation Time: 15 minutes

Cooking Time: 15 minutes

Servings: 2

Ingredients:

- 2 large tomatoes, sliced in half and pulp scooped out
- ½ cup broccoli, finely chopped

- 1 tablespoon unsalted butter, melted
- ½ cup cheddar cheese, shredded
- ½ teaspoon dried thyme, crushed

Directions:

1. Preheat the Air fryer to 355 degrees F and grease an Air fryer basket.
2. Mix together broccoli and cheese in a bowl.
3. Stuff the broccoli mixture in each tomato.
4. Arrange the stuffed tomatoes into the Air fryer basket and drizzle evenly with butter.
5. Cook for about 15 minutes and dish out in a serving platter.
6. Garnish with thyme and serve warm.

Nutrition:

Calories: 206, Fat: 15.6g, Carbohydrates: 9.1g, Sugar: 5.3g, Protein: 9.4g, Sodium: 233mg

Hummus Mushroom Pizza

Preparation Time: 20 minutes

Cooking Time: 6 minutes

Servings: 4

Ingredients:

- 4 Portobello mushroom caps, stemmed and gills removed
- 2 tablespoons sweet red pepper, seeded and chopped
- 3 ounces zucchini, shredded
- 4 Kalamata olives, sliced
- ½ cup hummus
- 1 tablespoon balsamic vinegar
- 4 tablespoons pasta sauce
- Salt and black pepper, to taste
- 1 garlic clove, minced
- 1 teaspoon dried basil

Directions:

1. Preheat the Air fryer to 330 degrees F and

grease an Air fryer basket.

2. Coat both sides of all Portobello mushroom cap with vinegar.
3. Season the inside of each mushroom cap with salt and black pepper.
4. Divide pasta sauce and garlic inside each mushroom.
5. Arrange mushroom caps into the Air fryer basket and cook for about 3 minutes.
6. Remove from the Air fryer and top zucchini, red peppers and olives on each mushroom cap.
7. Season with basil, salt, and black pepper and transfer into the Air fryer basket.
8. Cook for about 3 more minutes and dish out in a serving platter.
9. Spread hummus on each mushroom pizza and serve.

Nutrition:

Calories: 115, Fat: 4.1g, Carbohydrates: 15.4g, Sugar: 4.8g, Protein: 6.7g, Sodium: 264mg

Baked Plums

Preparation Time: 25 minutes

Servings: 6

Ingredients:

- 6 plums; cut into wedges
- Zest of 1 lemon, grated
- 10 drops stevia
- 2 tbsp. water

- 1 tsp. ginger, ground
- ½ tsp. cinnamon powder

Directions:

1. In a pan that fits the air fryer, combine the plums with the rest of the ingredients, toss gently.
2. Put the pan in the air fryer and cook at 360 °F for 20 minutes. Serve cold

Nutrition:

Calories: 170; Fat: 5g; Fiber: 1g; Carbs: 3g; Protein: 5g

Chocolate Mug Cake

Preparation Time: 15 minutes

Cooking Time: 13 minutes

Servings: 1

Ingredients:

- ¼ cup self-rising flour
- 3 tablespoons whole milk
- 1 tablespoon cocoa powder
- 5 tablespoons caster sugar
- 3 tablespoons coconut oil

Directions:

1. Preheat the Air fryer to 390 ^{0}F and grease a large mug lightly.
2. Mix all the ingredients in a shallow mug until well combined.
3. Arrange the mug into the Air fryer basket and cook for about 13 minutes.
4. Dish out and serve warm.

Nutrition:

Calories: 729, Fat: 43.3g, Carbohydrates: 88.8g, Sugar: 62.2g, Protein: 5.7g, Sodium: 20mg

Chocolate Soufflé

Preparation Time: 15 minutes

Cooking Time: 16 minutes

Servings: 2

Ingredients:

- 3 ounces semi-sweet chocolate, chopped
- ¼ cup butter
- 2 tablespoons all-purpose flour
- 2 eggs, egg yolks and whites separated
- 3 tablespoons sugar
- ½ teaspoon pure vanilla extract
- 1 teaspoon powdered sugar plus extra for dusting

Directions:

1. Preheat the Air fryer to 330 degrees F and grease 2 ramekins lightly.
2. Microwave butter and chocolate on high heat for about 2 minutes until smooth.

3. Whisk the egg yolks, sugar, and vanilla extract in a bowl.
4. Add the chocolate mixture and flour and mix until well combined.
5. Whisk the egg whites in another bowl until soft peaks form and fold into the chocolate mixture.
6. Sprinkle each with a pinch of sugar and transfer the mixture into the ramekins.
7. Arrange the ramekins into the Air fryer basket and cook for about 14 minutes.
8. Dish out and serve sprinkled with the powdered sugar to serve.

Nutrition:

Calories: 569, Fat: 38.8g, Carbohydrates: 54.1g, Sugar: 42.2g, Protein: 6.9g, Sodium: 225mg

Grilled Peaches

Preparation Time: 10 minutes

Cooking Time: 10 minutes

Servings: 2

Ingredients:

- 2 peaches, cut into wedges and remove pits
- ¼ cup butter, diced into pieces
- ¼ cup graham cracker crumbs

- ¼ cup brown sugar

Directions:

1. Arrange peach wedges on air fryer oven rack and air fry at 350 ^{0}F for 5 minutes.
2. In a bowl, put the butter, graham cracker crumbs, and brown sugar together.
3. Turn peaches skin side down.
4. Spoon butter mixture over top of peaches and air fry for 5 minutes more.
5. Top with whipped cream and serve.

Nutrition:

Calories – 378 Protein – 2.3 g.Fat – 24.4 g.Carbs – 40.5 g.

Cream of Tartar Bread

Preparation Time: 50 minutes

Servings: 6

Ingredients:

- 1 egg
- 3/4 cup sugar
- 1½ cups flour
- 1/3 cup butter
- 1/3 cup milk
- 2 zucchinis; grated
- 1 tsp. vanilla extract
- 1 tsp. baking powder
- 1/2 tsp. baking soda
- 1½ tsp. cream of tartar

Directions:

1. Place all ingredients in a bowl and mix well.
2. Pour the mixture into a lined loaf pan and place the pan in the air fryer
3. Cook at 320 °F for 40 minutes Cool down, slice and serve.

Quick 'n Easy Pumpkin Pie

Servings: 8

Cooking Time: 35 minutes

Ingredients

- 1: 14 ounce can sweetened condensed milk
- 1 large egg
- 1: 15 ounce can pumpkin puree
- 1 9-inch unbaked pie crust
- 1 teaspoon ground cinnamon
- 1/2 teaspoon fine salt
- 1/2 teaspoon ground ginger
- 1/4 teaspoon freshly grated nutmeg
- 1/8 teaspoon Chinese 5-spice powder
- egg yolks

Directions:

1. Lightly grease baking pan of air fryer with cooking spray. Press pie crust on bottom of pan, stretching all the way up to the sides of the pan. Pierce all over with fork.

2. In blender, blend well egg, egg yolks, and pumpkin puree. Add Chinese 5-spice powder, nutmeg, salt, ginger, cinnamon, and condensed milk. Pour on top of pie crust.
3. Cover pan with foil.
4. For 15 minutes, cook on preheated 390oF air fryer.
5. Remove foil and continue cooking for 20 minutes at 330 ^{0}F until the middle is set.
6. Allow to cool in air fryer completely.
7. Serve and enjoy.

Nutrition:

Calories: 326; Carbs: 41.9g; Protein: 7.6g; Fat: 14.2g

Leche Flan Filipino Style

Servings: 4

Cooking Time: 30 minutes

Ingredients

- 1 cup heavy cream
- 2-1/2 eggs
- 1 teaspoon vanilla extract
- 1/2: 14 ounce can sweetened condensed milk
- 1/2 cup milk
- 1/3 cup white sugar

Directions:

1. In a blender, blend well vanilla, eggs, milk, cream, and condensed milk.
2. Lightly grease baking pan of air fryer with cooking spray. Add sugar and heat for 10 minutes at 370 ^{0}F until melted and caramelized. Lower heat to 300 ^{0}F and continue melting and swirling.

3. Pour milk mixture into caramelized sugar. Cover pan with foil.
4. Cook for 20 minutes at 330 ^{0}F.
5. Let it cool completely in the fridge.
6. Place a plate on top of pan and invert pan to remove flan easily.
7. Serve and enjoy.

Nutrition:

Calories: 498; Carbs: 46.8g; Protein: 10.0g; Fat: 30.0g

Shortbread Fingers

Servings: 10

Preparation Time: 15 minutes

Cooking Time: 12 minutes

Ingredients

- 1/3 cup caster sugar
- 1 2/3 cups plain flour
- ¾ cup butter

Directions:

1. In a large bowl, mix together the sugar and flour.
2. Add the butter and mix until a smooth dough forms.
3. Cut the dough into 10 equal-sized fingers.
4. With a fork, lightly prick the fingers.
5. Set the temperature of air fryer to 355 degrees F. Lightly, grease a baking sheet.
6. Arrange fingers into the prepared baking sheet in a single layer.

7. Arrange the baking sheet into an air fryer basket.
8. Air fry for about 12 minutes.
9. Remove the baking sheet from air fryer and place onto a wire rack to cool for about 5-10 minutes.
10. Now, invert the short bread fingers onto wire rack to completely cool before serving.
11. Serve.

Nutrition:

Calories: 223, Carbohydrate: 22.6g, Protein: 2.3g, Fat: 14g, Sugar: 6.7g, Sodium: 99mg

Toasted Coco Flakes

Preparation Time: 8 minutes

Servings: 4

Ingredients:

- 1 cup unsweetened coconut flakes
- 2 tsp. coconut oil
- ¼ cup granular erythritol.
- ⅛ tsp. salt

Directions:

1. Toss coconut flakes and oil in a large bowl until coated. Sprinkle with erythritol and salt. Place coconut flakes into the air fryer basket.
2. Adjust the temperature to 300 Degrees F and set the timer for 3 minutes.
3. Toss the flakes when 1 minute remains. Add an extra minute if you would like a more golden coconut flake. Store in an airtight container up to 3 days.

Nutrition:

Calories: 165; Protein: 1.3g; Fiber: 2.7g; Fat: 15.5g; Carbs: 20.3g

Notes

Printed by BoD™in Norderstedt, Germany